OTHER BOOKS BY MAX LUCADO:

INSPIRATIONAL

3:16
A Gentle Thunder
A Love Worth Giving
And the Angels Were Silent
Come Thirsty
Cure for the Common Life
God Came Near
God's Story, Your Story
Grace
Great Day Every Day
Facing Your Giants
Fearless
He Chose the Nails
He Still Moves Stones
In the Eye of the Storm
In the Grip of Grace
It's Not About Me
Just Like Jesus
Max on Life
Next Door Savior
No Wonder They Call Him the Savior
On the Anvil
Outlive Your Life
Six Hours One Friday
The Applause of Heaven
The Great House of God
Traveling Light
When Christ Comes
When God Whispers Your Name

FICTION

Christmas Stories
The Christmas Candle

BIBLES (GENERAL EDITOR)

Grace for the Moment Daily Bible
The Lucado Life Lessons Study Bible
Children's Daily Devotional Bible

CHILDREN'S BOOKS

A Max Lucado Children's Treasury
Do You Know I Love You, God?
God Forgives Me, and I Forgive You
God Listens When I Pray
Grace for the Moment: 365
Devotions for Kids
Hermie, a Common Caterpillar
Itsy Bitsy Christmas
Just in Case You Ever Wonder
One Hand, Two Hands
Thank You, God, for Blessing Me
Thank You, God, for Loving Me
The Boy and the Ocean
The Crippled Lamb
The Oak Inside the Acorn
The Tallest of Smalls
You Are Mine
You Are Special

YOUNG ADULT BOOKS

3:16
It's Not About Me
Make Every Day Count
Wild Grace
You Were Made to Make a Difference

GIFT BOOKS

Fear Not Promise Book
For These Tough Times
God Thinks You're Wonderful
Grace for the Moment
Grace for the Moment Morning
and Evening
Grace Happens Here
His Name Is Jesus
Let the Journey Begin
Live Loved
Mocha with Max
One Incredible Moment
Safe in the Shepherd's Arms
This Is Love
You Changed My Life

THE
CHRISTMAS
CANDLE

MAX LUCADO

THOMAS NELSON
Since 1798

NASHVILLE   DALLAS   MEXICO CITY   RIO DE JANEIRO

Published in Nashville, Tennessee, by Thomas Nelson. Thomas Nelson is a registered trademark of Thomas Nelson, Inc.

Thomas Nelson, Inc. titles may be purchased in bulk for educational, business, fund-raising, or sales promotional use. For information, please e-mail SpecialMarkets@ThomasNelson.com.

Publisher's Note: This novel is a work of fiction. Names, characters, places, and incidents are either products of the author's imagination or used fictitiously. All characters are fictional, and any similarity to people living or dead is purely coincidental.

ISBN: 978-1-40168-994-0 (2013 Repackage)

Library of Congress Cataloging-in-Publication Data

Lucado, Max.
    The Christmas candle / Max Lucado.
      p. cm.
    ISBN: 978-1-59554-147-5 (regular edition)
    ISBN: 978-1-59554-278-6 (SE)
    1. Christmas stories. I. Title.
    PS3562.U225C45 2006
    813'.54—dc22

                                2006000706

Printed in the United States of America

13 14 15 16 17 18 RRD 6 5 4 3 2 1

FOR GREG AND SUSAN LIGON:

CELEBRATING THE LUMINATION
YOU BRING TO SO MANY

Dear Reader,

December evenings in Texas resist the holiday spirit. They tend to be balmy and warm, more tropical than polar. But I remember one in 2004 that cooperated. A chill was in the air. Winter was creeping southward. We bundled up in our winter coats and drove to the nearby high school for a Christmas banquet.

Families sat at round tables adorned with wreaths. Each wreath held a candle as its centerpiece. We drank wassail, ate turkey, and—the highlight of the night—we listened to the high school choir sing a rendition of holiday songs.

THE CHRISTMAS CANDLE

It might help to know that the school is Episcopalian, with strong Anglican roots. The choir director cherished the old hymns—less "Chestnuts" and "Rudolf" and more "Silent Night" and "Hark! The Herald Angels Sing."

It was delightful. As the choir sang and the families listened, I enjoyed that all-too-fleeting feeling of "all is right with the world." I stared at the candle on our table. As it flickered, I thought of candles that have done the same at a thousand other Christmases. And as I enjoyed the moment and watched the candle, a story began to take shape. A candle maker in the English Cotswolds. A nineteenth century village of simple people in need of a miracle. By midnight, I had sketched the story on paper: *The Christmas Candle*.

The story became a book and the book has lifted spirits for seven Christmases.

And now, with this new release, we hope the candle story will touch a whole new generation. Thanks to Tom Newman and the fine folks of Impact Productions, the movie version of *The Christmas Candle* is complete. The film was produced, directed, and acted by some of the finest talent in the UK: Director John Stephenson, Director of Photography Mike Brewster, and cast members including Hans Matheson, Samantha

Barks, Lesley Manville Sylvester McCoy, John Hannah, Barbara Flynn, and James Cosmo. This film also marks the acting debut of Susan Boyle.

I couldn't be more pleased. The screenplay, written by Candace Lee and Eric Newman, builds on the original story, adding characters and scenes and embellishing others.

When Denalyn and I visited the movie set in England, we were transported back in time. As we stepped into a centuries-old church and walked the cobblestone streets of the Cotswolds, we saw characters in period garb, horse-drawn wagons, and merchants with their eighteen hundreds' wares. We quickly and happily abandoned our modern habits. What a delightful experience! And what an honor to be a part of capturing this golden era slice of British history. May the charm of the nineteenth century Cotswolds inspire everyone who sees the film.

May the reading of this story delight your imagination. And may the ever-present message of Christmas encourage every seeker.

The light of the candle still flickers.

Max

PROLOGUE

December 1664

Light exploded in the small house, making midnight seem as daylight. The bearded candle maker and his wife popped up in bed.

"Wh-wh-what is it?" she said, trembling.

"Don't move!"

"But the children?"

1

"They're sleeping. Stay where you are!"

The wife pulled the blanket up to her chin and took a quick look around the shadowless room: children asleep on the floor, the table and chairs resting near the hearth, tools piled in the corner.

The candle maker never shifted his wide-eyed gaze. The figure wore a singular flame: a heatless tongue stretching from ceiling to floor. His form moved within the blaze: a torso, head, and two arms. He reached out of the radiance and extended a finger toward a rack of hanging candles. When he did, the couple squeezed together and slid farther back in the bed.

The husband mustered a question: "Are you going to hurt us?"

The visitor gave no reply. He waited, as if to ensure the couple was watching, touched one of the candles, and then vanished.

The room darkened, and the just-touched candle glowed. The man instinctively reached for it, stepping quickly out of bed and across the room, grabbing the candle just as the light diminished.

He looked at his wife. She gulped.

"What just happened?" she asked.

"I don't know."

He moved to the table and sat. She hurried to do the same.

"An angel?" she wondered aloud.

"Must be."

He placed the candle on the table, and both stared at it. Neither knew what to say or to think.

The next morning found them still sitting. Still staring.

Their children awoke, so they ate breakfast, dressed warmly, and walked the half mile up Bristol Lane to St. Mark's Church for the celebration of the final Sunday of Advent. The candle maker gave the rector extra candles for the Advent service but kept the angel-touched candle in his coat pocket. He started to mention the visitation to the reverend but stopped short. *He won't believe me.*

The couple tried to concentrate on the sermon but couldn't. Their minds kept reliving the light, the angel, and the glowing candle.

They shared a pew with a young mother and her two children, all three disheveled and dirty. The couple knew her, knew how her husband, a servant to a baron, had died a month before in a hunt.

After the service the widow described her plight to them. "We have little food left. Enough for a few days."

The chandler's wife reached into her husband's coat pocket for a coin. When she did, she felt the candle. She handed both to the young mother, inviting, "Light this and pray." As the young mother turned to leave, the wife looked at her husband and shrugged as if to say, "What harm?"

He nodded.

They spoke some about the candle over the next few days but not much. Both were willing to dismiss it as a dream, perhaps a vision.

The Christmas Eve service changed that. It began with a time of blessing-sharing. Anyone in the congregation who wanted to give public thanks to God could do so. When the rector asked for volunteers, the young mother stood up. The same woman who, days earlier, had appeared unkempt and hungry. This night she beamed. She told the congregation how a wealthy uncle in a nearby county had given her a farm as a gift. The farm was a godsend. She could live in the house and lease the land and support her family. She looked straight at the candle maker and his wife as she said, "I prayed. I lit the candle and prayed."

The couple looked at each other. They suspected a connection between the candle and the answered prayer, but who knew for sure?

CHAPTER 1

AFTERNOON

May 4, 1864

"I just think it odd that Oxford would assign its top student to a village like Gladstone," Edward Haddington said to his wife, Bea. A broad-shouldered man with a brilliant set of dark eyes and full, gray eyebrows, he wrestled to button the waistcoat over his rotund belly.

Equally plump Bea was having troubles of her own. "How long since I wore this dress?" she wondered aloud. "Must I let it out again?" Then louder, "Edward, hurry. He's due within the hour."

"Don't you think it odd?"

"I don't know what to think, dear. But I know we need to leave now if we don't want to be late. He arrives at half-past one."

The couple hurried out of the small gabled house and scurried the half mile south on Bristol Lane toward the center of the village. They weren't alone. A dozen or more villagers walked ahead of them. By the time Edward and Bea reached the town commons, at least half the citizens of Gladstone, some sixty people, stood staring northward. No one noticed the white-haired couple. All eyes were on the inbound wagon.

The driver pulled the horses to a halt, and a young man stood to exit. He bore beady eyes, a pointed chin, and his angular nose seemed to descend forever before finding a place to stop. With a tall hat in his hand and a black coat draped on his shoulders, Rev. David Richmond surveyed the crowd. Edward detected a sigh. "We must appear odd to him," he whispered to Bea.

She cupped an ear toward him. "What?"

He shook his head, not wanting to risk being overheard.

A goggle-eyed locksmith, so humped from filing he had to greet the guest with a sideways, upward glance, extended the first hello. Next came a short farmer and his Herculean, simpleminded son. "He can clean the windows in the church," the father offered. "He did for Reverend Pillington." A mill worker asked Reverend Richmond if he liked to fish. Before he could reply, a laborer invited the minister to join him and his friends at the pub.

"Let the man breathe, dear people. Let him breathe." The citizens parted to let

Edward extend his hand. "A fine welcome to Gladstone, Reverend. Did you enjoy the carriage ride?"

Reverend Richmond had ample reason to say yes. Spring had decked the Cotswolds in her finest fashions. Waist-high stone walls framed the fields. Puffy flocks dotted the pastures. Crows scavenged seeds from melting snow. May clouds passed and parted, permitting sunlight to glint off the shallow creeks. England at her best. Yet the minister replied with an unconvincing, "It was pleasant."

Edward picked up the clergyman's bag and led him through the crowd. "We'll deposit your things at the parsonage and let you freshen up. Then I'll leave you with the Barstow family for tea."

As the crowd dispersed, the reverend nodded and followed his hosts toward the manse. It sat in the shadow of St. Mark's Church, which was only a stone's throw from the center of town. The hoary, dog-toothed Norman tower stood guard over the village. Edward paused in front of the church gate and invited, "Would you like to take a look inside?"

The guest nodded, and the three entered the grounds.

A cemetery separated the church from the road. "To preach to the living, you have to pass through the dead," Edward quipped.

"Edward!" Bea corrected.

Reverend Richmond offered no reply.

The walls of the path through the cemetery were, at points, shoulder high, elevating the headstones to eye level. The newest one lay beneath the tallest yew tree near the church entrance and marked the burial place of St. Mark's former rector. Edward and Bea paused, giving Richmond time to read the inscription:

REVEREND P. PILLINGTON

MAN OF GOD.

MAN OF FAITH.

MAN OF GLADSTONE.

OURS, BUT FOR A MOMENT.

GOD'S FOREVER.

1789–1864

"This month we'd have celebrated his fiftieth year at the church," said Bea.

"When did he die?" the reverend asked.

"February," Edward answered. "Hard winter. Pneumonia took him."

"God took him," Bea altered.

Edward nodded. "We dearly loved the man. You'll find his fingerprints throughout the valley. He taught us to trust, to pray. He even taught me to read and write."

Bea chimed in. "Edward here was a diligent student. Come ahead. Let's step inside."

The heavy doors opened to the rear of the sanctuary. Three shafts of stained-glass sunlight spilled through tall windows. "My grandfather helped install those," Edward offered. He strode the five short steps to the baptismal font and motioned for the reverend to join him. "Dates back two centuries," Edward said, running a finger along the limestone. "My ancestors were all baptized here. In fact, my great-great—Bea, how many 'greats' is it?"

She placed a finger to her lips. "Let the reverend meditate."

Edward apologized with a wave and stepped back.

One aisle separated two groups of ten pews. A lectern faced the seats on the left, and a pulpit presided over the church from the right. Brass organ pipes climbed the chancel wall behind the pulpit, where two sets of choir benches faced each other.

"My Bea plays the organ," Edward boasted.

The clergyman didn't respond. He made the short walk to the front and stopped at the first of the five swaybacked stone steps leading up to the pulpit. A thick Bible and empty glass rested on the stand.

"Been vacant since February," Edward offered.

Reverend Richmond turned with a puzzled look. "No minister filled in?"

Bea shook her head. "Only on occasion.

21

Gladstone is too remote for most clergymen. But we've gotten by."

"Right," Reverend Richmond said, suddenly ready to leave. "Shall we move on?"

Bea extended a hand. "I'll go home and prepare some dinner. Reverend, enjoy your visit to Gladstone."

Edward showed the minister the parsonage and waited outside until he was ready for the first appointment of the afternoon.

Charles Barstow cut an imposing figure standing in his doorway: thick shoulders, long face, hollow cheeks flanked by snow-white sideburns, and eyebrows as thick as hedges.

As Edward presented the reverend, he explained, "Charles runs the local mercantile. Need boots, hats, or hammers? He can help you."

Richmond noted the fine house: ivy framed its dormers; jasmine and roses charmed the porch.

"Charles, I'll leave him in your care," Edward said.

"Fine."

Mr. Barstow's wife joined him at the door and escorted them to a table in the inglenook next to the fireplace. She stood much shorter than the two men, her head level with her husband's shoulders. She was overdressed, better attired for the theatre than for tea. She attempted a sophisticated air, as if wanting to be in, or at least from, some other town. "Tell me," she nasaled, pausing after each word. "How is life in Oxford?"

Her husband sighed and motioned for the minister to sit. "I understand you grew up in London."

"I did."

"My family is from Putney—some time back, however. And yours?"

"Kensington. I'm the first to leave the

city, actually. That is, if I do. I shall be the first in our family not to serve the royal household in generations."

"Oh." Mrs. Barstow perked up. "What is your connection?"

"My father is a barrister."

"My, my," Mrs. Barstow admired.

The Barstows' granddaughter, Emily, joined them at the table.

Reverend Richmond was grateful to see someone closer to his age, even more thankful to see someone so pretty. Emily's curled brown locks fell to her shoulders. Her warm hazel eyes ducked from his glance. He looked away, equally embarrassed.

"I hear you have no wife," her grand-mother said.

Emily blushed. The reverend caught the hint but didn't reply.

Mr. Barstow redirected the conversation with questions about Oxford, but his wife was not easily deterred. At the next pause, she jumped in. "Our dear friend's niece will marry next week. As for us, we have no plans."

Emily, who still hadn't spoken, shot a glance at her grandmother.

"That's good to know," Reverend Richmond offered, then corrected himself. "I mean, it's nice that your friend is marrying, and, well, I hope you will . . . or your granddaughter will marry soon as well. If she wants to, that is."

"Tell me, Reverend." Charles spoke, to the minister's relief. "What do you think of the candle?"

"The candle?"

"The Gladstone Candle."

"I, uh, can't say I've heard of it."

The three Barstows shared wide-eyed glances.

"You've never heard of the candle?" Mrs. Barstow asked.

"Or the candle maker?" Mr. Barstow added.

"Or the Christmas miracles?" Emily completed.

"No," the reverend admitted, feeling that he'd missed a long conversation.

The three looked at him with eyes reserved for a sumptuous meal, each wanting to eat first. "Well, let me tell you—" Mrs. Barstow volunteered.

"Maybe I should do that," her husband interrupted. But a knock at the door stopped him. He stood and answered it.

"I knew if I didn't come, you'd forget to bring him to our house," said a friendly, round-faced woman.

Mr. Barstow turned toward the minister.

"This is Sarah Chumley. She'll take you to your next visit."

Reverend Richmond gave her a puzzled look. Sarah chuckled. "You've apparently met my twin, Bea Haddington. Don't even try to tell us apart. People who have known us for years still grow confused."

Richmond stood, thanked his guests. Mrs. Barstow spoke again. "I'll be glad to finish what we started, Reverend."

Did she mean the candle or the courting? He didn't know and didn't dare ask. He turned and smiled a half smile, grateful to be leaving.

Sarah Chumley was as cheerful as the

morning sun, was wide-waisted, and blessed with plump cheeks that flushed with rose and rendered eyes into half moons at the slightest smile. She escorted the minister down the street, two houses past St. Mark's Church. She paused at the parsonage that separated her home from the church building. "This is the . . ."

"I know, the parsonage. I've already dropped off my bags."

"Reverend Pillington lived here for half a century. A dear man. Scratchy after souls, he was." She paused as if enjoying a memory, then invited, "Come. Mr. Chumley looks forward to meeting you."

She led Reverend Richmond through a chest-high gate and a golden garden of goldilocks and buttercups. Wisteria stretched over the honey-colored cottage walls, and bright red paint accented the front door. Her husband opened it, not to let them in, but to let a patient out.

"Keep it wrapped, now, Mr. Kendall. Apply the liniment like I showed you, and"—placing a hand on the old man's shoulders, Mr. Chumley winked—"don't you think it's time you let the younger people birth the lambs?"

"I'm as spry as I ever was," the man countered. "Hello, madam," he added.

31

"Afternoon," Sarah greeted. She and the reverend stepped aside so the injured shepherd could pass. "My husband's the village alchemist, closest thing Gladstone has to a doctor. Try to find a villager he hasn't treated—you won't find one."

Mr. Chumley was a slight man, bespectacled and short. But for a crown of gray, he would have been bald. "Come in, come in!" He clasped his hands together. "Been looking forward to meeting you." He led them through the pharmacy in the front of the house to the parlor, where the reverend entered into his second conversation of the afternoon. He soon discovered that Mr. Chumley and the former rector had been fast friends. The two men had shared tea, problems, and long winters; but, curiously, they hadn't shared matters of faith. "I leave things of God with God," Mr. Chumley stated pointedly.

"I can respect that," Reverend Richmond said.

"You can?"

"Of course I can. Theology has changed since your former rector studied."

The reverend noted Sarah's furrowed brow but continued. "God keeps his distance, you know. He steps in with Red Sea and resurrection moments, but most of the time he leaves living life up to us."

"I've never heard such thoughts," Sarah said, joining the two men at the table.

"Nor have I, but I've had them," Mr. Chumley agreed. "I treat the body and leave the treatment of the soul to those who believe one exists." He reached across the table and placed a hand on Sarah's. "Like my wife."

"I still pray for him, however."

"And I still attend services . . . though my mind does wander."

The Chumley visit proved to be Reverend Richmond's most enjoyable of the day. He had dabbled in chemistry, and Mr. Chumley enjoyed debating theology. They took turns

34

on each subject until the peal of St. Mark's tower clock prompted Sarah to interrupt. "I promised Bea to have you at their house within the hour."

"I'll take him," Mr. Chumley volunteered. He donned a hat and grabbed his cane as the minister expressed thanks to his hostess, and the two stepped outside onto Bristol Lane, where horse hooves clicked on egg-shaped cobblestones, small thatched-roof houses lined the street, and villagers gave generous greetings.

"Good day, Mr. Chumley, Reverend," offered a seamstress carrying yards of cloth.

"Hello there, Mr. Chumley," saluted

35

a farmer with mud-laden boots. "Those Epsom salts are helping the missus right well. Reverend, good to see you."

As they passed the town commons and the center cross, Mr. Chumley spoke about his in-laws, Bea and Edward Haddington. "The village treasures them. Not just because of the candle, mind you. They are dear, dear folk."

"What is this candle?" Reverend Richmond asked. "Mr. Barstow mentioned it to me as well."

The question stopped Mr. Chumley in his tracks. "You don't know about the candle?"

"No."

He removed his hat and scratched his head. "It's best that I let Edward tell you about it."

"And why is that?"

"He's the candle maker."

Chapter 2

EVENING

May 4, 1864

Clad in his finest homespun Sunday coat, Edward Haddington was standing beneath the sign that read CHANDLER.

"He's all yours," Mr. Chumley said.

Edward smiled and reached up to wrap an arm around Reverend Richmond's shoulders. "Don't worry, my friend. We aren't eating in my shop. I was just checking a few matters."

Edward said good-bye to his brother-in-law and led the minister next door, explaining as he walked, "My father and his father lived in the shop. I grew up there. But when I married, I promised Bea a house. She never could adjust to the smell of the candle shop. The tallow, you know. When her friends stopped coming over for tea . . . a change was needed." The two paused in front of the slate-roofed home.

"Our dwelling belonged to a tailor. When he died, his widow moved to Chaddington and sold it to us. What do you think?"

"Seems small." The reverend had to bend his neck to enter, lest he hit his head. The entire cottage consisted of one room. A table and four chairs sat to the right and a wrought-iron bed just beyond them. Two rockers rested in front of the fireplace, where a heating kettle filled the house with the smell of oxtail soup.

"Welcome to our home, Reverend. Won't you join us at the table?"

Reverend Richmond turned to see Bea, her silvered hair swept under a bonnet and glasses resting on her nose.

For the third time in one afternoon, the young man took a seat and began to eat.

They drank beer and ate soup and just-baked bread.

Edward was never one for small talk. He went directly to his question. "How is it that you've come to Gladstone?"

"Excuse me?"

"Mr. Barstow says you excelled in your studies."

The reverend arched an eyebrow. "Well, yes, I did quite well."

"You seem awfully bright for our village. Seems you would be assigned to a, well, how would you say it, Bea . . . a more sophisticated parish? We're simple folk."

"Forgive us, Reverend," Bea interjected.

"We don't mean to pry. We've never needed a new rector."

"Wouldn't you be better suited for a large church?" Edward persisted. "Perhaps in London? Don't you have family there?"

"No openings," was the reverend's terse reply.

Edward looked at Bea. She tilted her head as if to say, "Enough on this topic."

Edward looked away.

Bea proposed another question. "What do you find interesting about our village?"

Reverend Richmond stroked his beardless chin and remained silent. Edward got the impression that he was having a hard time coming up with anything. "The candle," he finally answered. "I'm curious about the candle."

Edward leaned forward. "Are you now? And what do you know about it?"

"Only that everyone keeps bringing it up."

"Are you sure you want to hear its history?" Bea asked.

"Why, of course."

"Perhaps we best fill our glasses, then."

As Bea poured, her husband lit his pipe and began to relate the details of Gladstone's favorite topic. "We need to go back a long way. I'm the seventh Haddington to make candles for Gladstone. The sign over the shop door? My grandfather made and hung it."

"Could use some paint," Bea added.

"My great-grandfather built the kiln. His great-grandfather, Papa Edward, migrated from Scandinavia in the 1650s. He built the shop and was the first Haddington to live in Gladstone. He was also the first to see the Christmas Candle."

"What do you mean, he *saw* the candle?" Reverend Richmond asked.

Bea spoke up. "We know less than we'd like about its origin. We'd know more had Edward's father not drowned in Evenlode River. It was a hard day, a hard time.

Edward was sixteen, still an apprentice. He was not fully trained yet. A bit too young to run the shop, but what choice did he have?"

Edward shrugged. "Mother and I did the best we could. And, in time, we did fine. I married Bea and buried Mother, and Gladstone settled down to another generation of candle buying."

He leaned back in his chair and puffed on his pipe as though he'd finished the story. Indeed, he thought he had. Bea had to jog him. "Edward, tell him about the Christmas Candle."

"Oh, of course. Yes, well, as Bea said, some of the details died in the river along with my father. But what I and all of Gladstone know is this.

"Papa Edward had passed a bitterly cold Saturday evening dipping candles for the Sunday service. Being the night before the final Sunday in Christmas Advent, he'd made more than usual. To this day I still do. We stand them in the windowsills and give them to the choir to hold as they sing. We've always enjoyed yuletide services and large church crowds during December. Is it the same where you're from, Reverend? Why, I remember one year when Reverend Pillington arranged for a chorus from St. John's at Chadwick to join us. Bands of

49

folks from three and four miles away came to sing the old, old songs."

He leaned forward and, with twinkling eyes and a bouncing head, sang a verse:

"Peace and goodwill 'twixt rich and poor!
Goodwill and peace 'twixt class and class!
Let old with new, let Prince with boor
Send round the bowl, and drain the glass!"

"Edward." Bea placed a hand on his. "The candle."

"Oh yes. The candle. Where were we?"

"The night before the final Sunday in Advent," Reverend Richmond aided.

"Right . . . Papa Edward and his wife were sound asleep when brightness exploded in the room. You would have thought a curtain had been yanked opened at noonday. A bonfire couldn't have been brighter. They sat up and saw a glowing angel. They watched him touch one of the candles and then disappear. Papa Edward grabbed it, looked at his wife, and the two spent the rest of the night wondering what had just happened."

"They had no idea what to think, Reverend," Bea continued. "They went to Sunday services saying nothing about the angel's visit. They feared people would think they were crazy. Before they left, however,

Mrs. Haddington gave the candle away. Touched by the plight of a young widow, she gave her the candle and urged her to light it and pray."

Edward picked up the story. "Each Christmas Eve church members are invited to stand and share a blessing. Well, imagine who stood first that year?"

"The young woman?" asked the reverend.

"She was a changed person. A generous uncle had provided for her needs, and Grandmother and Grandfather Haddington wondered about a connection between the candle and the gift, but they drew no conclusion."

Edward took a drink from his glass. When he did, Bea spoke up. "Half by hope and half by obligation, they continued to hang extra candles each eve of the final Advent Sunday. Then, after a quarter of a century, the December night glowed, and an angel touched another candle. Papa Edward gave it to a shepherd who was searching for his son. The father found the son, shared the news at the Christmas Eve service, and Grandmother and Grandfather knew something special was happening."

The reverend shifted uneasily in his chair. "And you credit God for this?"

"Who else?" asked Edward.

"You realize, of course, that these could all be coincidences."

"Indeed they could," Edward conceded. "But two hundred years have passed. Every quarter of a century an angel has touched one candle. Every prayer that was offered over the candle was answered."

"The Christmas Candle has become legendary," Bea interjected, "and so have the Haddington candle makers. Even when the region had other chandler shops, the angel only and always came to Papa Edward's descendants. The citizens of Gladstone have anticipated each candle maker's child the way the rest of England awaits a royal heir, which brings us to the hard part of this story." She looked at Edward. "God gave us only one child, a son. He was born to us late in life and died from cholera when he was twenty."

"I'm sorry to hear that. Was he married?"

"That he was. His wife died several months later in childbirth."

"My goodness. One tragedy followed the other."

"It did. Indeed, it did."

Edward noted this first ray of warmth from the reverend. His guard, for just a few moments, was lowered.

"And your grandchild?" Richmond asked.

Edward chose to veil his reply. "As you can see, Bea and I are alone. We're both in our seventies; we won't be having any more children."

"Does that mean the angel visits stop with you?"

"We assume so."

Richmond began reviewing the facts, counting them with his fingers. "The angel comes once every twenty-five years?"

Edward nodded.

"He touches one candle?"

"So far."

"And that candle has power?"

"No, God has the power. The candle is just the . . . Bea, what did you call it?"

"The vessel."

"Yes, the vessel."

The young minister crossed his arms and looked out the window.

"You find the story hard to believe?" Bea asked.

Reverend Richmond cleared his throat and looked back. "It's not the type of event you hear about often."

"No," Edward agreed, "far from it."

"How long since the last visit?"

Edward looked to Bea and let her answer the reverend. "Twenty-four years."

"Twenty-four? That means this is the . . ."

"Yes, this is the year," she agreed.

"Goodness. No wonder everyone's talking about the candle."

The conversation ended soon after that. Nothing else seemed worthy of mentioning.

Reverend Richmond spent the night in the care of the soft-spoken churchwarden who had welcomed him at the parsonage. His Gladstone tour continued the next day. He met a farmer who showed him his flock. ("Purebred Cotswold sheep. My rams are famous.") And a retired tailor, inquisitive and cautious. ("Some of us were hoping for an older minister, you know.")

All in all, the villagers could not have been more friendly . . . or more untitled, rural, and backward. (One farmer asked Reverend Richmond if he'd ever delivered a lamb.) No match for an academician like himself.

He returned to Oxford the following day and awaited the next opportunity: the call from London, Southampton, or at least Bristol.

The don made it clear: no other options were coming. "Given the problems you've had, Gladstone is your only option."

"Gladstone doesn't fit me," he said, shrugging.

The Gladstonians held the same opinion. "Not quite right for us," was Barstow's tactful comment in his note to the Oxford don. The citizens returned to their routine, hoping for someone older, married—seasoned. A pastor with thick skin for the winters, a warm heart for farmers, and an open mind for the mystery of Christmas miracles and angel-touched candles.

He never came.

Reverend Richmond came.

He arrived in June. June labored into July. Summer cooled into autumn. Apple trees dropped fruit and then leaves. Maples turned a rusty tint, and blackthorn bushes produced their purple sloe berries. Early October felt the first freeze, and Gladstone's new minister purchased an extra blanket from Barstow's Mercantile.

As he made his selection, Emily Barstow watched. When he looked up, she blushed and looked away.

In the church vestment box, Reverend Richmond found a warmer cape to wear in the pulpit. It was this robe that he donned the first Advent Sunday in December, the day he refused to preach about the candle.

The young mother pulled the blanket over the face of her infant son. Even seated inside the train, she felt the chill of the December air.

"Ticket?"

She looked up to see the uniformed conductor.

"Oh yes." She'd forgotten to keep it handy. Reaching over her sleeping child, she found the ticket in her purse. The conductor checked it and handed it back.

THE CHRISTMAS CANDLE

"We'll warm up as the train leaves the station," encouraged the lady in the adjacent seat. She was matronly in appearance: gray hair peeking from beneath a bonnet, wrinkled face still red from the chill. "Long trip for you and the baby?"

"All day," Abigail said.

"I'll keep you company, then." The lady looked around the crowded car. "Lots of travelers. Busy season."

The young mother nodded, cradled her son closer, and looked out the window at the sea of travelers. All wore coats and hats; most carried bags or children. Everyone was in a hurry to go somewhere. The train lurched, and Abigail grabbed the seat, then smiled at her neighbor.

"Jerky things, these trains," the woman sympathized.

Iron wheels slowly rolled the locomotive, mother, and child out of Paddington Station and into the city. Buildings passed, signs blurred, and Abigail felt moisture form in the corner of her eyes. She looked down at her sleeping son and spoke softly so no one would hear. *"Are we doing the right thing, little man?"* Then, as if answering for him, she said, *"What else can we do?"*

She sighed and reached into her bag and extracted a large brown envelope. She looked at the address, ran a thumb across her printed name, removed the letter, and did what she'd done a dozen times in the last twenty-four hours. She unfolded it and stared at the words. She thumbed away another tear.

"Are you all right?" asked the lady.

Abigail nodded but didn't look up.

65

"This letter. I, uh, I can't read. But my landlord read it to me. So I was just looking at it."

"Would you like me to read it to you?"

Abigail smiled. "I would like that very much." She handed her neighbor the paper and looked down into the face of her child and listened as the woman read.

Chapter 3

FIRST SUNDAY
OF ADVENT

December 4, 1864

As Edward took his seat in the church, he heard snatches of conversations, enough random sentences to reveal the topic on everyone's mind.

"If I get the candle, I know what I'll pray for . . ."

"I hear Edward already knows who he'll give it to . . ."

"Do you suppose he'd talk to me about it?"

Edward was relieved to see Bea take her seat at the hundred-year-old organ. Now the service would begin and the whisperings cease. People followed the cue of the ten-member choir as they stood to sing "Come, Thou Almighty King." Limestone walls echoed with "Praise God, from whom all blessings flow . . ." As the congregation sang, Edward looked out the window and spotted the reverend walking from the parsonage through the cemetery. As he leaned into the bracing wind, he held the neck of his coat closed and then loosened it as he neared the doors of the church.

THE CHRISTMAS CANDLE

I wonder what Reverend Richmond has prepared to say to us, Edward considered. He knew what Reverend Pillington would have said. He had understood the cherished place the candle held in the lives of Cotswold villagers. They endured difficult days: crawling out of bed on dark, cold mornings; closing the barn after the sun had set; sewing by the light of the fire; laboring through weeks of rainy, sunless seasons. The former rector had understood the life of the villagers and how the legend of the candle always lifted their spirits. Were he preaching today, he'd speak of surprises and angels and fresh hope in the midst of dark Decembers. He'd speak about the candle.

"No. I can't do that," the young minister had told Edward earlier in the week. "I'm not Pillington. I don't preach about candles. People don't need old wives' tales."

"But this is . . ."

"I know. This is the year. But I give people practical help and solid facts. I stay away from mysteries."

"You don't believe, do you?"

"I believe in the Bible. I believe in the church. I believe in God. But I see no reason to promote superstitions or raise false hopes."

"Don't you think God can work however he chooses?"

"I believe God worked, and the rest is up to us."

So as the singing ceased and the choir took their seats, Edward shifted in his pew, anxious to hear what the reverend would say.

The congregation heard the click of Richmond's boots as he ascended the stone steps to the pulpit. He looked nervously over his flock and unfolded his notes with the ease of a suitor asking for a maid's hand in marriage.

He spoke of Christmas kindness and neighborly love and Christian charity. Most other churches would have appreciated the message. But not the parishioners of St. Mark's. As they left the building, some refused to shake the reverend's hand. Others did so with disappointment. "The candle?" they asked. "Did you forget?"

Edward tried to hide his frustration but had trouble doing so. "Your sermon could have been better, Reverend." He then followed Bea as she and Sarah exited the nave.

"Nothing!" Sarah whispered. "He didn't say a word, not one word!"

"Perhaps it's for the best," Bea replied. "People are already so . . ."

"Persistent," Edward finished for her.

"Persistent, indeed," Bea continued.

CHAPTER 4

MONDAY

December 12, 1864

An outside noise interrupted Edward's sleep. He opened his eyes and stared into the dark, not wanting to climb from beneath the covers. The bell in the ancient tower struck the five o'clock hour with lingering vibrations, as if its teeth were chattering in the belfry.

"It's cold," he muttered as he snuggled up to his wife.

He was almost back to sleep when he heard the noise again. This time Bea heard it too.

"Edward," she whispered, "did you hear that?"

"Probably just a hedgehog."

"Go and see."

"It's freezing, Bea." But even as he protested, he knew he had to go. He grumbled and obliged. He grabbed his coat off the back of the chair, threw it on over his nightshirt, and opened the door.

Moonlight illuminated a shivering hump against the wall of his house.

"Bea! Someone is out here!"

"Actually, Edward, there are two of us."

"James, Elizabeth, what are you doing?" Edward asked.

"Waiting on you," the woman answered, making ghosts with her breath.

By now Bea, wrapped in her bed's blanket, stood next to her husband. "Come in, you two," she urged. "You'll die of chill."

They were only too happy to oblige.

As the couple settled in by the fire, Edward begged for an explanation.

"Can we warm up a bit first?" James requested with trembling chin.

In short order Bea filled four cups with tea. The unsolicited guests wrapped their hands around the warmth and sighed as they sipped.

James and Elizabeth Clemly ran the Queen's Tavern south of town in a century-old building they rented from the lord of the manor in Chipping Campden. The two served as the first line of hospitality for Gladstone-bound travelers. As he offered hay and rest to the horses, she filled pints and plates in the pub. This morning they had walked the length of Bristol Road in the predawn darkness.

Edward's curiosity mounted as the couple's cups emptied. He was soon drumming the table with his fingers. "What is this all about?" he finally asked.

Elizabeth looked at James. He bore a heavy salt-and-pepper beard and a mop of matted hair. He pulled off his hat and wrung it like a wet rag and looked toward Elizabeth, who urged him on by pressing her lips together.

"The missus and I have a request."

A request? Edward was puzzled.

James squeezed his hat again and shifted forward in his chair. "Me and Elizabeth were wondering . . . You know I never ask anything of you, Edward. I always pay what I owe."

"That you do," the chandler offered. "So how can we help you?"

"My luck ran out. A couple of months back I was rollin' quite nice in a game in the pub. All cards were comin' my way. I knew I couldn't lose, so I bet it all. I even bet the next six months' earnings. Every shilling."

Elizabeth groaned.

James looked down at the floor and said, "I lost."

"You lost?"

"Everything. Elizabeth still has a few pence, but that's all we have left."

THE CHRISTMAS CANDLE

Edward scratched his head. "Well, I can't say that I know much about cards, but if you're looking for some advice, I know a fellow in Bibury—"

"The candle!" Elizabeth blurted.

"The candle?" Edward asked.

"Edward," offered Bea in a firm tone, "the Christmas Candle. After the angel's visit. They would like us to give them the candle."

"We're broke, Edward," James said. "The lord of the manor wants his rent money, and, well, he has been wanting it for two months now. He's talking eviction."

"Oh, I don't think . . . Surely he would listen to you."

"He won't. We've tried. Edward, you're our only hope."

"I see." Edward looked at Bea for a few moments, then at the floor and back to his friend. "Well, you know, James, your need poses a bit of a problem." He cleared his throat. "We're still a week from the angel's coming, and many people have already stopped by."

Bea kept her hand on Elizabeth's as Edward continued his explanation. The same explanation he had given the farmer whose oldest son had broken his leg just before harvest, leaving the farmer short-handed. "I left a year's earnings in the field. I could use a miracle."

The same explanation he had given to Widow Leonard. Too old to work, she lived on what she took in from renting out the back of her house. She told Edward how new tenants were hard to find and how there wouldn't be enough money to buy coal for the rest of the winter.

"The Smith family needs help too," Edward continued. "They have twins, you know, sweetest little things. Have you seen them? Why, when Mrs. Smith walked in my shop with one in each arm—"

"Edward," Bea interrupted, once again bumping him back on track.

"Oh yes. Well, she fears for their health.

And then Phineas Austen dropped by. Let's see, Bea, was it last Friday? Saturday? No matter. His wife is losing her sight. You've seen her. She's using a cane now. All those years of making . . . What is it she makes, dear?"

"Bonnets, Edward. She stitches lace on bonnets."

"She's going blind, and that's what I thought Phineas wanted to discuss. But he is more concerned about their son. He's in trouble with the law, and they fear"—by now Edward was lighting his pipe—"that he may"—he stopped midsentence to take a couple of puffs from his pipe—"end up in prison."

James stared at the floor, and Elizabeth leaned her forehead into her fingers.

"And who was it that came yesterday after Sunday services, Bea?"

"I believe you've made your point, Edward."

"I have?"

"Yes, you have," James assured. "Many requests. Many requests. I just thought . . . We just thought that, well . . ."

Bea slid her chair next to Elizabeth's. "We do understand. And we will pray. That's all we can do. Pray. We don't know why God has given us this gift. But we pray that he will direct us. He did before."

Elizabeth nodded. "I think often of Charles Barstow," she said. "Twenty-five years ago—before you gave him the candle—he was as directionless as a ship with no rudder. Now look at him. He is a fine man, fine indeed. You chose well."

"God led us then, and he will again. Now," Bea said, "we've all got work to do."

Bea and Edward stood in the doorway as their visitors departed. Edward wrapped an arm around his wife, and she asked, "What are we going to do? So many people need the candle. How can we decide who to give it to?"

Edward said nothing.

"I've been thinking," Bea said.

"About what?"

"That we could use the candle for ourselves. Our need is as deep as they come."

Edward shook his head slowly. "I don't know, dear. Our family has always given it away."

"But has any Haddington faced what we're facing?"

Edward reached across and took her hand. "We'll see. We'll see."

Abigail passed the morning the way she had begun it: seated on a train, holding her baby, pondering the words of the letter. London streets gave way to England countryside. Even under the blanket of winter, the hills maintained their charm. Abigail could see villages in each valley marked by tall towers, gabled roofs, and clustering elms.

It felt good to be going home. She just wished for different circumstances.

THE CHRISTMAS CANDLE

Her fingers twisted the corner of her baby's blanket as if her hands needed something to hold on to. Will it be the same? *she wondered.*

CHAPTER 5

SATURDAY EVENING

December 17, 1864

Guests occupied every corner of the Barstow parlor. With full bellies and filled glasses, they lingered long after the meal. Charles Barstow discussed politics with two guests from Upper Slaughter. Mr. Chumley listened politely to an elderly friend's complaints about arthritis. Mrs. Barstow relayed the latest gossip on romance and marriage.

Bea and Edward had declined the invitation to dinner. Everyone understood why. This was, after all, *the* night. The eve of the final Advent Sunday. They had preparations to make, a guest to receive.

The reverend, however, had accepted the Barstows' invitation.

"You came." Emily brightened as he arrived. In six months the two had shared no more than six sentences, but he had noticed her watching him.

"I saw you last week joking with the Johnson children," she noted as the two talked.

The rector smiled, pleased to be caught in an act of kindness. "I, uh, I enjoy them. Their mother is sick, you know."

"I know."

"The twelve-year-old asks me many questions."

"Does he?"

"Great questions. Questions of faith and God."

"Like?"

The reverend's voice animated just slightly. "The other day he mused, 'How do we know we aren't butterflies dreaming we are humans?'"

Emily smiled. "And you told him?"

"I told him, 'That's a good question.'"

The two laughed, and his face softened.

"You should do that more often," Emily urged.

"Do what?"

"Laugh!" She clapped her hands. "I never see you laugh."

Richmond looked down at his tea.

"Do you find Gladstone dull?" she ventured.

"Dull? Of course not . . ."

Her eyes betrayed her disbelief, so he adjusted his response, admitting, "At first, yes. I confess, my heart was set on going elsewhere."

"London?"

"I was raised there. My father is a friend of the bishop. It made sense that I serve in London."

"But . . ."

"London was not an option."

"I thought you had family connections."

"Other factors were considered." As soon as the words left his mouth, the reverend's face flushed, and he looked away. Emily waited for him to continue, but he didn't.

"The candle." Emily finally changed the subject. "You must know everyone is upset that you aren't saying anything about the candle in your sermons."

"Yes, I know."

"I don't understand. Don't you believe in it?"

"I can't encourage false hope. I want no part of disappointing people."

"And the candle disappoints people?"

"How can it not? One candle. A village of needs. God would not single out one person and ignore the others. It's not fair."

Emily replied with measured words. "Perhaps he singles out one person to show the others what he can do."

The reverend started to speak, then stopped. "Can I think about that?"

She smiled her yes.

"Excuse me, but Sarah and I are bidding our farewells," Mr. Chumley interrupted.

"Our bedtime nears. We aren't young like you," Sarah added. "Have you had a good evening?"

"Quite." The minister nodded.

"Tomorrow's a working day for you, Reverend. Are you ready with a sermon?"

"Indeed it is, and that I am."

With a wry smile Mr. Chumley looked at the young minister. "And all this talk about the candle. Are you converted yet, or do you still stand with me on the cynic's side of the fence?"

"Mr. Chumley," Sarah interrupted her

husband, "the hour is too late to wade into another discussion. Let's get your hat and cane."

"I suppose we'll know more soon. Good night."

"I suppose we shall," Reverend Richmond agreed. "Good night to you both."

The young couple watched the Chumleys leave.

After some time Richmond spoke. "I suppose I should leave as well."

"Perhaps we could visit again?" Emily risked.

He started to speak, stopped, then continued. "I'm not who you think I am, Emily.

I'm not as hard as the village thinks, nor am I as good as you think. I've made mistakes and . . ."

"And mistakes are to be put in the past."

"Emily?" Mr. Barstow called from the door. "Can you join us? Our guests are leaving."

"Certainly, Grandfather," she answered but turned to the minister first and with a slight smile repeated, "in the past."

CHAPTER 6

LATE SATURDAY NIGHT

December 17, 1864

A dancing fire warmed Edward's shop, and two hanging lanterns illuminated it. Bea kept him company, rocking and knitting in the corner.

He enjoyed talking as he worked, and Bea didn't mind listening.

"Did I tell you about the merchant from

Ironbridge I met at the pub?" He measured twine as he talked, cutting it into ten-inch strips.

"I don't think you did."

"He told me about Thomas Trevor, a chandler who works near the coal mines. He employs four workers twelve hours a day. With the five of them, they produce nearly five thousand candles a week."

"I can't imagine the sort."

"Why, the most I can ever sell in Gladstone is a hundred a week. Although here I am preparing thirty for tomorrow alone."

"Tomorrow's different."

Edward completed his cutting and began wrapping the twine on one of the three rods of his dipping rack.

"This Trevor fellow has a tool he calls the 'nodding donkey.' It rotates like an indoor windmill, holding six racks, with each holding thirty or so candles by the wicks as they dry. He even has a machine for cutting the wicks. He sets a dozen spools in a tray, stretches the strings across a table, and lowers the blade on them. He calls it a guillotine."

"I can see why."

"You haven't heard the half of it. Trevor makes some of the candles green."

Bea lowered her needles and looked up. "Who wants green candles?"

"Mine owners do. It seems that some of their workers find the tallow tasty and have taken to chewing it. Others think the wax protects their throats from the dust. For whatever reason, miners chew the candles, eating up the mine owner's property and profits."

"But green candles?"

"The color sticks to the mouth. When a foreman spots a worker with green lips and tongue, he boots him out."

Bea shook her head and placed her knitting in a basket. "It's not worth a candle."

"Indeed not."

"I'm going to the house, but I'll be back."

"Bundle up."

Edward tied the last of the strips of twine to the rack, took it by either side, and walked across the shop. He lowered the thirty strings into the tub of hot tallow long enough for the waxy substance to cling and then lifted them out. As he repeated the process again and again, the candles began to thicken, and his thoughts began to wander.

Blame it on the late hour or significant night or both, but Edward grew nostalgic, reflective. "How many times have I done this? How many hours in this shop?" he said aloud to no one but himself. "My, it's been good. Good wife, friends . . . faith."

Cold air rushed into the room. He turned and saw Bea standing in the doorway. The fireplace glow silhouetted her frame. Her face was left in shadows, and for a moment he saw her as she had looked at age twenty-five. Slim figure. Her hair burnt orange, as bright as a summer sunset, reminding him of the night fifty years earlier when they had first seen the angel.

Edward's reverie was interrupted by the sound of his wife's voice. "Edward? Did you hear me? Would you like some tea?"

"Yes. That would be nice." Edward, content with the width of the candles, suspended the rack on eye-level ceiling hooks in the center of the shop.

Bea handed him a cup, and the two stood looking at the rack.

"Remember fifty years ago?" he asked. "The first candle we gave?"

"To Reverend Pillington. How could I forget?"

"He and I were the same age."

"He was a year younger perhaps. But he was so desperate to believe."

Edward nodded. "I remember feeling odd giving a candle of faith to a man of faith."

"Purveyors of hope need it the most."

"God blessed him. And blessed Gladstone through him." Edward lowered his tea. "May he rest in peace."

The candle maker cleaned the tallow tub and stoked the fire. Only then did he notice that Bea had left the shop again.

She returned with a bottle and held it up as she closed the door. "Apple wine?"

"A gift from Elizabeth?"

"Nice to be bribed."

She filled two cups and handed one to him. He lifted his as a toast. "To the last candle."

"To the last candle."

THE CHRISTMAS CANDLE

They again took their seats by the fire, and for a time neither spoke.

"The house is quiet this year," said Bea.

"Painfully so."

Bea turned toward her husband. "Can we talk about the candle again? Do we have to give it away? Would it be so bad if we kept it for ourselves?"

"Now, Bea. I don't know if it is intended for us."

"Maybe, since it's the last one, this candle is a gift to the Haddington family. Maybe?"

"Perhaps. The Lord knows we could use a miracle." He lit his pipe, and the two rocked in silence.

"Staying awake?" she finally asked.

"Why certainly," he pledged.

Good intentions, however, gave way to weary bodies. Little by little their eyelids drooped and heads lowered. Before the fire had embered, their heads rested, chins on chests, and the candle maker and his wife were sound asleep.

The light woke them. Brilliant, explosive, and shocking light. December midnight became July noonday. Edward needed a moment to come to his senses. He couldn't remember why he was sleeping in a chair and not in his bed. As Edward rubbed his eyes with the heels of his hands, Bea nudged him.

Her whisper had force. "Edward! The angel!"

He looked straight into the light, squinting as if looking into the sun. He distinguished a silhouette.

The angel lifted an illuminated hand and paused as if to make certain the couple was watching. He took a step in the direction of the rack. Edward and Bea leaned forward. The angel touched a candle toward the end of the third row—and

117

then disappeared. The candle glowed for a few seconds against the now-darkened room.

As the light diminished, Bea urged, "Edward! The candle!"

If only he had kept his eyes on it. If only he hadn't looked away to see where the angel went. If only his foot hadn't gone to sleep. Then the calamity might have been averted, but it wasn't.

Edward took a step on his tingling foot and lost his balance. As he fell face forward, he thrust one hand high in the air, hoping to grab the just-touched candle. Instead, he hit the rack and knocked it off the hooks, sending thirty candles—thirty identical candles—flying around the room.

Edward looked up at Bea. Bea looked down at Edward. Horrified. They sprang to their feet and raced around the shop, examining candles in the hope that one of them might contain a glimmer of light. None did.

After a few moments both plopped into their chairs, hands full of candles. Neither had the slightest notion which candle had been touched by the angel.

Bea burst into tears. "Now what? We have thirty candles. One of them is special, and we don't know which!" She buried her face in her hands. Edward stared at the floor.

As the shock wore off, Bea spoke up. "You'll have to make a new batch for tomorrow's Advent service. We can't risk giving away the angel candle."

"I will. We'll save this batch until we know what to do."

Bea set the thirty candles in a basket, and Edward got busy in the shop.

CHAPTER 7

SUNDAY

December 18, 1864

After church the next morning, Edward and Bea were the center of attention.

"Visitors last night?"

"Any candles to distribute this week?" Wink.

"Come see me tomorrow, Bea. I'll make biscuits." Wink. Wink.

Later that afternoon Edward decided to go for a walk. "I need to get outside for a while, dear. Would you like to come?"

Bea declined. "You go ahead."

But as he left the house, she stopped him. "Take these." Bea handed him the basket of candles from the night before.

"Why?"

"I don't know. God may tell you what to do with them."

Edward stopped by the livery stable to greet his old friend Adam Patterson. Adam was tall and lean and ever happy and could make Edward feel as if the day revolved around his arrival. This day, however, there was no cheerful shout from within the stables, no slap on the back or offer of tea and biscuits. Edward found Adam in a horse stall, seated on a stool, leaning against a wall.

"Adam?" Edward hurried to his side. "What is wrong?"

His friend didn't look up. "It's my head, Edward. It pounds and pounds."

"When did this start?"

"Last week."

"Why didn't you tell me?"

"You've been busy with the candle."

"Have you talked to Mr. Chumley?"

"I have. He has no solution." Adam

looked up for the first time. "My father, Edward. Remember?"

Edward remembered. Years before, Adam's father had complained of the same symptoms and had died within a week.

Still looking at Edward, Adam said, "My friend, I know I ask much. But God must have guided you to me for a reason. Tell me. Do you still have the candle?"

The candle maker pulled a stool next to Adam and sat. "I do," he answered. He had the candle; he just didn't know where. Yet how could he admit this to Adam? The pain had paled his friend's face and left his hands trembling. Edward sighed and made his decision. He reached into his basket and handed Adam a candle. "Take this, my friend. God will hear your prayers."

Adam's eyes misted with gratitude. Edward's heart clouded with confusion. What had he done? How dare he give hope? But how dare he not? Adam was his friend, and, who knows, he *might* have given his friend the Christmas Candle.

Edward requested, "Let's keep this our secret."

"Whatever you say."

After some time the candle maker left the livery stable and continued his walk. James Clemly spotted him on the street.

When the pub owner requested a moment to chat, Edward guessed the topic. "The lord of the manor needs his rent, and I need some help."

Edward motioned for James to follow, and the men stepped between two buildings. Having already given a candle at the livery stable, it seemed easier to do so again. James embraced him. Again Edward suggested secrecy. "Perhaps it's best that you not tell anyone."

"Sure," agreed the bright-eyed James. "The element of surprise, right?"

How will I explain this to Bea? Edward wondered.

He returned to the house and said little. He wanted to tell her what he had done but couldn't find the words.

"I'll be in the shop." He placed the candle basket on the table and walked out the door.

When Sarah dropped in for afternoon tea, Bea told her sister about the visitors and hint droppers. Sarah grew quiet. "Bea," she said, stirring her drink, "if I had any other options, I wouldn't trouble you. But I have none."

129

Bea extended her hand across the table and covered her sister's. "Sarah, what is it?"

"I married a dear man, Bea. He cares as much for me today as the day we married. But even after all these years and all our prayers, he still has no faith. His world consists of what he sees and touches." She paused to dab a tear. "We're living our autumn years, dear sister."

Bea nodded. "We're both living with unanswered prayers, are we not?"

Sarah squeezed Bea's hand. "What am I doing, sharing concerns with you? You have enough troubles of your own."

"Sarah," Bea spoke firmly, "don't worry

about us. Something is on your mind. What is it?"

"I'm thinking of the candle, dear sister. Is there any way . . ."

Bea sighed. "Let me tell you what happened Saturday night." She described the light and the touch of the angel. When she told about Edward's stumble, the two sisters laughed until they cried. And as they filled the house with happiness, Bea made a decision. She stopped short of telling her sister the whole story. She didn't mention that they didn't know which candle the angel had blessed. Bea reached into the basket. "Here, Sarah. For you. For your husband's faith."

131

Sarah clutched the gift to her chest and beamed, her face awash with tears.

"Perhaps it's best to tell no one for now," Bea said.

"Of course."

The two stood and embraced. As she watched her sister leave, Bea asked herself, *How will I explain this to Edward?*

She was asking herself the same question an hour later as Emily Barstow walked quickly away from the shop, a candle tucked under her shawl. *She only wants the young reverend to notice her. How could I not give her hope?*

THE CHRISTMAS CANDLE

Standing at the doorway to their home that evening, Edward and Bea could see the villagers walking toward the church.

"Should we go join them?" Bea asked.

"Let's stay home. I need to tell you what I did today." He told it all. Adam's headaches, James's request. "I gave candles to them both. Have I done a horrible thing?"

Bea said nothing. Edward thought she was angry. "What have I done?" he asked.

"Exactly what I did," she confessed and then shared the details of Sarah and Emily. "People will be so angry, so hurt. All our friends will think we deceived them."

"But we didn't mean to mislead anyone, dear."

"I know, but we did. What will they think when their prayers go unanswered? We should have kept all the candles."

"And leave the special candle in the basket?"

"We can't do that, either."

"Bea, we did the only thing we could. We gave candles, hoping to give the right one."

"So what do we do now? Give them all?"

Edward sighed. "Do we have a choice? How else can we be sure that someone will receive the Christmas Candle?"

"True." She nodded, then smiled. "Edward, now we can light a candle too."

"I suppose we can," he said.

Abigail knew little about Oxford, but she didn't need to know much. The walk from the train station to the carriage house was brief and direct. The gray cloud cover and fog muffled the noonday sun. She was tempted to find a room and rest. But she knew better. Wait too long and she might lose her courage.

She made her way through the winding streets and boarded the covered cart. Left to her own means, she could

never afford the passage in a carriage.
But the courier who had delivered the
letter had delivered money as well.

Other passengers dozed as the wagon
bounced. She couldn't. Her mind kept
returning to the words of the letter . . .
By now she knew them almost by heart.

CHAPTER 8

MONDAY

December 19, 1864

Early the next morning Reverend Richmond knocked on the Haddingtons' door. Bea answered it. "Merry Christmas, Reverend. Won't you come in?"

"Edward, I need to speak with you about this candle business," he began. His tone was less than cordial. "People expect me to mention it in the Christmas Eve service."

"Yes, they do."

"To ask the recipient of the candle to stand."

"That's the tradition."

"How can I? This is superstition. Have you seen the parishioners? They are counting on the candle to help them . . . to save them . . . to rescue them . . ."

"It's not the candle that can save them, Reverend. It's the Giver of it."

"This is disastrous."

Edward and Bea had never seen him so worked up.

"You should preach like this," Edward offered.

"Edward," Bea buffered.

"What do you mean?" The reverend frowned.

"With passion. Your preaching could use some. A little pulpit fire never burned a church, you know. Why, Reverend Pillington . . ."

"I weary of hearing about Reverend Pillington."

The trio sat in embarrassed silence for a few moments. Edward finally spoke up. "What are you afraid of, Reverend? Afraid the prayers won't be answered or afraid they will?"

The young rector started to speak, then stopped.

Edward continued in soft yet firm tones. "The mystery of God unsettles us all, Reverend. But isn't mystery where God works? If he does only what we understand, is he God?"

He paused, inviting the rector to reply. He didn't. Nor did he look away. Edward opted for bluntness. "Do you fear that God will dash the faith of the people, my son? Or do you fear that he will stretch yours?"

Reverend Richmond's face softened for a moment. Then it hardened. "All this talk of angels and hope. Where will it lead us?"

"And your dismissal of miracles . . . Where will that lead us?"

The reverend started to object, but Bea placed a motherly hand on his and, for the first time, addressed him by his Christian name. "David, something burdens you. What is it?"

The young minister said nothing.

Edward leaned forward. "The first day we met I asked you why Gladstone. You seem groomed for the cathedral, a city like Gloucester, not a country parish. You never answered that question. Perhaps this would be a good time to do so."

Reverend Richmond pressed his two

hands into a tent and leaned his lips into them. After several moments he lifted his eyes and began to speak.

"Four of us were at a pub. It was a year ago . . . a year this month. We were celebrating the coming holidays. The winter night was cold, the ale was good, and the fire was warm. So we drank. We drank until we, well, we became foolish, foolish and loud.

"Patrons told us to be quiet. The pub owner threatened to throw us out. I told him my father's name and position and dared him to do so. He didn't hesitate.

"Next thing I knew we were standing outside, bracing against the cold. The wind was bitter and I was too. The man had humiliated me in front of my friends. Embarrassment prompted me to do something I'll regret for the rest of my life.

"I saw an empty delivery wagon in the street, still hitched to its team. I jumped on, grabbed the reins, and told my friends to go with me. They hesitated . . . so I prodded. 'What are you, afraid?' They finally climbed up.

"I was imagining a fast ride, a few laughs. We'd have the wagon back at the pub before anyone missed it."

The Reverend looked down.

"What happened?" Edward asked.

"Something horrible. I had no business

147

handling a wagon. The wind was strong, I was drunk and inexperienced. I slapped the reins and off we went. I feigned being in control. My buddies knew better. They told me to slow down, go back. But no, I had my pride.

"A narrow bridge crosses the Thames a mile north of the pub. The road bends sharply just before the crossing. The turn demands care on a clear day with a good driver. A drunk one on a dark, icy night has no hope. I missed it entirely. When I knew what was happening, I pulled up, but it was too late. The horses, the wagon, we all plunged over the edge of a steep ravine and fell fifteen feet into the water.

"All of a sudden I was fighting to stay afloat. Three of us made it to the river's edge. We looked frantically for George, our friend. We stomped up and down the bank, crying out his name, crying out to God.

"We had to abandon the search—we were freezing. We found a house and got help. They located his body the next morning."

The trio sat in silence for a long time.

Bea was the first to speak. "I'm so sorry, son. You must be heartbroken."

"More than you could imagine. I was so stupid, so childish. I got what I deserved. But my friend . . . he didn't deserve to die. I suppose that's why I see God in the fashion I do."

He turned and looked straight at Bea, lower lip quivering. "God could have helped. He should have helped. I used to think he hears us when we pray. But I prayed that night. With all my heart . . . now, I don't know anymore."

"This is how you ended up in Gladstone?" Edward asked.

Richmond nodded. "We should have been expelled. My father intervened, however. But the don made it clear I would never know the likes of a preferred pulpit. I guess Gladstone is my penance."

"Or," Edward adjusted, "Gladstone is where you find forgiveness."

Bea looked at her husband. "It's all right that we tell him, don't you think?"

"About Abigail?" he answered.

The clergyman looked at her. "Tell me what?"

"We didn't tell you the whole story. The fact is, our granddaughter used to live with us . . . until a year ago. She ran away last January. We think she is in London; a friend saw her there last spring."

"Why did she leave?"

"She made a mistake she must have thought we couldn't forgive," Bea explained.

"We've tried to find her," Edward added. "Believe me, we've tried."

Bea walked across the room and lifted a candle from the basket. "I guess we all need Christmas miracles, don't we, David?"

She handed the candle to the minister. "Take this, my son. You need some light."

He smiled, "I don't think I should . . ."

"Just take it."

He placed the candle in his coat and stood to leave. As Edward opened the door, he made a request. "Follow the tradition in the Christmas Eve service. Who knows what might happen?"

Edward and Bea watched him walk away; then Edward closed the door.

THE CHRISTMAS CANDLE

"Bea," Edward invited, "we have one more candle."

She knew his thoughts and smiled. He set the candle in the holder; the two sat at the table and prayed. They prayed for forgiveness, faith, and a young girl in a large city.

CHAPTER 9

CHRISTMAS EVE

December 24, 1864

By the end of the week, the candle basket was empty. Thirty hopeful Gladstonians guarded their candles and secrets and looked for a miracle. A ten-year-old girl prayed for her arguing parents. The family of a sailor prayed for his safe arrival. A wife prayed for her husband to sober up. Reverend

Richmond had never seen so many week-day visitors stopping to pray.

As the Christmas Eve service drew nigh, however, Edward and Bea expressed occasional bouts with doubt.

"What will people do to us when they realize we gave them common candles?" Bea asked.

"Do you think your uncle in Preston could give us a place to live?" Edward teased, only partly in jest.

"Credibility. Friends. Candle shop. We could lose it all," Bea listed.

"Still, we have to attend the service, if for no other reason than to explain."

THE CHRISTMAS CANDLE

"They won't believe us," Bea lamented.

Edward planned his words and mentally rehearsed them over and over. By Saturday night he was ready. They waited until the singing had begun before stepping out into the cold night and walking to the church for the Christmas Eve service. The streets were empty; everyone was in St. Mark's.

"Well, dear husband, only God knows what awaits us."

"At least one person will be happy to see us."

The couple found space on the back pew and took a seat. Strands of garland draped between the windows, and a row of flames flickered in each sill. The children's nativity play was in full swing. Emily Barstow had organized the cast and props. The locksmith played one of the wise men, as did Adam from the livery stable. A homemade doll rested in the manger, and a lamb kept bumping it over with her nose. Laughter and applause bounced off the church's stone walls.

Reverend Richmond began his welcome. "We thank the ladies who cleaned the floors, our men who repaired the door. We appreciate the Haddingtons for the window candles." Several heads swiveled and looked at the couple. Edward and Bea kept their eyes on Reverend Richmond.

"This is my first Christmas Eve service with you," the reverend continued. "I understand that the church traditionally begins this gathering with testimonies and announcements of blessings. We have all been blessed, far more than we deserve. Yet I am told that among us sits one person who has benefited from an angel's touch." He paused, looked over the audience, and invited, "Could I ask that soul to stand?"

Edward and Bea gulped. She closed her eyes. He took her hand and whispered, "We'll be all right, dear." He bowed his head and offered a silent prayer. *Lord, these are your people, your flock. Look with kindness upon this moment.*

He heard the congregation begin to murmur. "What is this?" someone said aloud. Another wondered, "How can this be?" Then a third, "What is going on?" Edward assumed the worst. *No one is standing.*

But when he and Bea opened their eyes, they couldn't believe what they saw: people standing all over the sanctuary.

Reverend Richmond took a step back from the pulpit. "I don't understand. Why so many of you?"

Villagers began asking for permission to say a word. The reverend called on a farmer on the front row. "You know me, Edward," he turned and spoke across the crowd. "I can't resist the bottle. But since you gave me the candle, I've been here, in prayer, each evening. Why others are standing, I can't say, but I haven't touched a drop in four days."

"Reverend," requested another man, "may I?" The young minister nodded, and James stood. "My landlord and I have been at odds for months about the rent. But last Sunday, Edward gave me the candle. The missus and I prayed, and yesterday the landlord came to me and said, 'Who am I to make demands? Apart from God's mercy, I would have nothing,' and then he gave me a clean slate and said he'd extend more credit if I needed it."

Adam, from the livery, spoke next. "Like you, Reverend, I'm bewildered by this response. I know this, however: my head is better. Not healed, but better."

The Widow Leonard rose. "I rented out the back of my house."

A man stood up next to her. "And I found a place to live."

Even Emily raised her hand. Looking directly at the minister, she said, "I'm not sure he notices me, but the more I pray, the more I know God does."

Blessing after blessing.

"My husband's been gone since summer. But he promises he's back to stay."

"Our son is back from sea."

"Mr. Barstow hired me at the mercantile. I don't have to sell my farm."

Edward and Bea watched with wide eyes and listened with happy hearts. Finally, after a harvest of good news, Edward stood. "I need to say something." He walked down the aisle, turned, and looked into the weathered faces of the villagers.

Digging his hands deep in his pockets, he began, "The night the angel came something happened that no one expected."

He told them the story, every detail: the

deep slumber, the glowing light, the tingling foot, and the fall. (All chuckled at this point.) "Who has the real Christmas Candle? Only God knows, but he does know. And I know he uses the mistakes of stumblers." He cast a knowing glance at the reverend. "And he has heard our prayers.

"Perhaps we trusted the candle too much. Perhaps we trusted God too little. So God took our eyes off the candle and set them on himself. He is the Candle of Christmas. And Gladstone? Gladstone is one of his Bethlehems. For he has come to us all."

A chorus of *amen*s boomed in the church.

"Bea, I've preached enough. Come to the organ. It's time to sing!"

Bea played every Christmas carol she knew, from "God Rest Ye Merry, Gentlemen" to "Hark! The Herald Angels Sing." Queen Victoria heard no sweeter music than St. Mark's did that Christmas Eve.

But midway through "Silent Night" the service came to a frightening halt. The entrance doors slammed open, and a disheveled man ran in screaming, "Help! Someone help!" Sudden air gusted, whipping the flames on back window candles. Singing stopped and a hundred heads turned toward the rear of the sanctuary.

Edward, with a clear view from his aisle seat, recognized the man as the driver of the coach wagon. He was a stark contrast to the worshippers—they, gleeful and warm; he, saucer-eyed and freezing. Ice clung to his beard and fear hung from his words. Grasping for breath, he sputtered, "One side of the bridge . . . Collins Bridge . . . it gave way."

Gladstonians gasped at the thought. "Are you hurt?" someone shouted.

"No . . . my passengers . . . they fell over the side. I looked for them, but it's too dark."

"They?" Richmond asked. He stepped up the aisle toward the man. "Who was with you?"

"A girl and her baby. The other passengers got off at Upper Slaughter. We should have stayed the night there, it's so cold and icy. But she insisted."

Richmond spun toward the front of the church. "Hurry. The creek is shallow. She may be all right. All able-bodied men come with me."

"I'll have a fire going in my house," Sarah volunteered.

"I have extra lanterns in my pub," shouted James.

"And I have more in my store," Barstow offered.

"Get them. Grab blankets and rope as

well," Richmond instructed. "We don't have a minute to waste. Adam, bring a wagon. This girl will be in no condition to walk."

"Certainly."

"Meet at the bridge! May God have mercy."

The moment the people said "amen," the midnight bells began to ring. Worshippers scurried into the frigid night under the commission of twelve chimes.

CHAPTER 10

MIDNIGHT

December 24, 1864

Clouds blocked stars and wind howled through the trees. Edward wrapped a scarf around his face and felt a stab of dread in his heart. *Could anyone survive this cold?* he wondered to himself.

He and Richmond were the first to leave St. Mark's. The reverend grabbed a lit lantern that hung by the exit and Edward followed. They hurried down Bristol Lane onto the muddy, wagon-wheel rutted road. Edward stayed a step behind his young companion, benefiting from the light and the windbreak. Neither spoke for the ten minutes it took to reach Collins Bridge.

They paused for a moment at the crossing. One of the corner beams, weakened from weather and wear, tilted forward causing the bridge to slope steeply toward the water. The wagon remained on the suspension, thanks to the two horses standing firmly on dry ground. Edward envisioned the young mother, struggling to hold on, and then falling over the edge.

"Hurry, Edward, let's search downstream."

A gust of wind picked up as the two walked toward the ravine. Edward heard voices behind him and turned to see another set of lanterns. He couldn't distinguish the carriers and didn't wait to try.

"We're going on the west side," he yelled. "You cross over!"

"We will!" It was Mr. Chumley.

Edward caught up with Richmond who was illuminating the slope with the lantern. "Be careful, Edward, it's muddy."

Edward tried his best but lost his footing and slid the five feet down the edge.

"I'm okay," he assured. "Just glad I wasn't holding the lantern."

"Indeed," Richmond agreed as the two began to slush their way along the bank.

"Any idea who the girl is?" Richmond yelled over the wind.

"No."

"Hello!" they cried. "Hello!" But they heard nothing.

The two were in the water as much as out of it. The steep slope and trees left them the slenderest path. The water soon soaked their boots, numbing their legs from the knees down. Richmond, with the lantern, led the way, careful not to advance too far ahead of Edward. He paused often to yell:

"Still there?"

"Yes, yes," Edward assured.

As it turned out, it was Richmond who took the fall. He ventured around a tree by stepping into the water, one hand on the trunk, the other holding the lantern. His foot slipped, and he and the lantern fell into the stream.

Edward saw the reverend splash and stopped in the abrupt darkness.

"I'm fine, Edward. I'm fine," he heard the reverend assure. Through the inky night Edward made out the form of Richmond struggling to his feet and back to the shore.

"We have no light," the reverend bemoaned. They heard the water rushing, leaves rustling, and then . . . from downstream, a call for help.

"Edward! Did you hear that?"

"I did."

The call came again. This time Edward responded. "We're coming!"

"But I can't see one step ahead of me!"

"Feel your way forward."

Richmond didn't budge. "I can't move. This is too familiar. The cold. The darkness. The water. Oh, God," he pleaded, "not again."

Edward placed a hand on his shoulder. "Don't give up on God, son."

Richmond folded his arms and shivered.

As he did he felt something in his coat. A candle. The candle Edward had given him earlier.

"Do you have a match, Edward?"

"A match?"

"I found a candle in my pocket."

"It will do no good," he told Richmond. "The flame can't withstand the wind."

"It may for a moment. And a moment of light is better than none!"

Edward reached for the matches he kept to light his pipe. "Let's lean together and block the wind!"

The two stood side by side as Edward struck the match. It flared, then disappeared.

"Closer! Stand closer to me!" the candle maker instructed.

Both men bent at the waist. Richmond held the candle as still as his shaking hands allowed. The match flame touched the wick, then expired.

"It's wet," Edward explained.

"One more time," Richmond urged.

Edward took another match, struck it, and held it toward the candle. Richmond cupped his hand around the wick. The flame held, dancing for a moment. "I think it's going to light."

It did more, much more. Before the two men could straighten, radiance exploded.

The light of a dozen torches pushed back the darkness. A bonfire couldn't have been brighter. Edward could see the wide eyes and dropped jaw of the reverend. "What is happening?" Richmond asked.

"A miracle is happening, son. Hurry, these lights tend to pass quickly."

Richmond reached the girl first. She was on the ground, huddled against a tree, clutching a bundle to her breast. "Looks like she was trying to find her way out," Richmond suggested. He squatted and placed a hand on the girl's shoulder. "Are you all right?"

No response.

"Is she alive?" Edward asked.

Richmond removed his glove, lifted her chin, and placed two fingers beneath her scarf. He scarcely breathed as he felt for a pulse. He never got one, but didn't need one. The girl groaned.

"She's alive, Edward."

Richmond turned his attention to the child. He lifted the blanket and placed a hand beneath the small nose. "This one is fine too. Sound asleep, likely better off than the mother."

Noises emerged from behind them.

"What is this light?" Barstow asked as he and four others hurried to help.

"An answered prayer, Charles," Edward smiled. "Let's get these two out of the cold."

THE CHRISTMAS CANDLE

Richmond rode in the back of the wagon with Mr. Chumley, the mother, and the child. They covered the two with blankets. Edward sat in front with Adam. The rest of the men hurried along behind.

True to her word, Sarah had a blazing fire with which to welcome them. "She's drifting in and out of consciousness," Chumley told her. "Must have hit her head."

"Let me have the baby."

Chumley handed his wife the child, and

he and Richmond carried the mother into the small parlor and seated her near the fire. Edward and Adam quickly followed. Within moments, all of Gladstone, it seemed, was in the room or on the porch.

Bea placed a warmed blanket on the girl's shoulders. "We'll let you rest a bit, then get you out of those wet clothes." As of yet, no one had seen the young mother's face. It was completely scarf-wrapped, leaving room only for a set of eyes that, Edward noticed, seemed to grow wider by the moment.

"There, there," motherly Bea comforted, offering a cup of tea. "This will help. Let me take your wrap."

184

Bea undraped the scarf as one unwraps a gift, and what Bea saw was the finest gift she could have imagined.

"Abigail!"

Edward leaned forward from the fire.

Sarah gasped.

Mr. Chumley shook his head, "It's Abigail."

"Abigail?" Richmond asked everyone.

"My granddaughter," Edward explained as he knelt by the chair and embraced his prodigal child. Bea joined him and, for the first time in too long, the three held each other and wept.

Abigail finally pushed back. "Papa, Grandmother . . . where is my baby?"

Sara handed her the child. Abigail slipped the blanket away from the baby's face. "I named him Edward."

Whispers of the news and name rippled across the room and out the door to the men on the porch.

Edward looked up and searched out the eyes of Reverend Richmond. "Looks like God still gives babies at Christmas," he winked.

"And light," the minister agreed. "He still gives light when we need it the most."

EPILOGUE

I know it's dark. I should be home within an hour," the store owner assured his wife over the phone. He stared out the window at the snow-covered cars. "But tomorrow is Sunday, and I want to take the day off. Put the baby to bed. I'll be home soon, and we'll finish decorating the tree. Besides, I only have four more boxes to empty."

"Okay, dear. I'll take care."

He hung up and returned to the task. He cut open the cardboard and placed the candles side by side on the shelf. Each box contained different shapes, and each shape went to a different section of the store. By the time he finished, the shelves were full, and the time was well past the hour he had promised to be home.

Rather than hurry out, however, he sat at the desk to pay a few bills. "I'll feel better getting these ready," he justified. But he made it only halfway through the stack when he leaned over the desk and fell sound asleep on his arm.

THE CHRISTMAS CANDLE

The next thing he knew, light exploded in the room. He sat up and rubbed his eyes. Ed Haddington gulped as the figure within the flame extended a finger toward one of the fat candles on the lower shelf . . .

Acknowledgments

Thanks to many friends for helping out on this book:

Art and Karen Hill, Casey Fast and Liz Heaney—Everyone should have such research trips, right? Thank you for everything!

The gracious folks at the Lord of the Manor Inn, Upper Slaughter, England—You embody the the charm of the Cotswold's.

Brian Bird and Michael Landon, Jr.—thanks for your creative input into this story.

And Andrea Lucado, more than a daughter this time, a co-writer. You've done for this book what you've done for my life—sweetened it with grace.

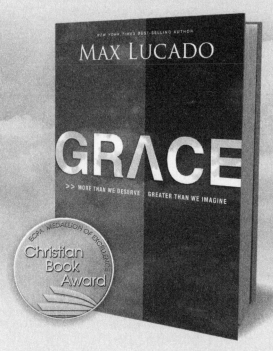
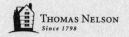

Inspired by what you just read?
Connect with Max.

Listen to Max's teaching ministry, UpWords, on the radio and online. Visit www.MaxLucado.com to get FREE resources for spiritual growth and encouragement, including:

- Archives of UpWords, Max's daily radio program, and a list of radio stations where it airs
- Devotionals and e-mails from Max
- First look at book excerpts
- Downloads of audio, video, and printed material
- Mobile content

You will also find an online store and special offers.

www.MaxLucado.com

1-800-822-9673

UpWords Ministries
P.O. Box 692170
San Antonio, TX 78269-2170

Join the Max Lucado community:

Follow Max on Twitter @MaxLucado
or at Facebook.com/UpWordsMinistry